I0059689

HOLD THE CHEESE!

Transforming Your Caller's Experience

Chester Hull

W̶A PRESS

Wizard Academy Press
Austin, Tx

Copyrights Page

Copyright © 2012 by Chester Hull
All Rights Reserved

Permission to reproduce or transmit in any form or by any means, electronic or mechanical, including photocopying and recording, or by an information storage and retrieval system, must be obtained by writing to the publisher at the address below:

Wizard Academy Press
16221 Crystal Hills Drive
Austin, Tx 78737
512.295.5700 voice 512.295.5701 fax
www.WizardAcademyPress.com

Ordering information:
To order additional copies, contact your local bookstore, visit www.prosoundusa.com/HoldTheCheese, or call 877.677.6768. Quantity discounts are available.

ISBN: 978-1-932226-86-7

Credits:
Cover by Daniel Agee - www.danieleagee.com

First Printing: April 2012

Copyright © 2012 Chester Hull All Rights Reserved

This is book wouldn't have been possible with out Roy Williams planting the seed in me, Michael Drew showing me how to write, Stephen Palmer showing me where to find the words, Paul Boomer, Dave Young, and Tom Wanek patiently reading rough drafts and encouraging me, and countless others asking "when will it be finished?". And I'm sure I left you out as well. So "thank you".

How to Use This Book

One of the challenging things about writing a book about sound is that sounds can't be read! So throughout the book, as I reference audio or video clips, you'll see a QR code nearby. It will look like this:

http://prosoundusa.com/Video

This QR code links to my online video introduction from Sunpop Studios. To hear the audio or see the video, simply use your Smartphone to scan the QR code. Each time you see a QR code, go ahead and scan it. It will add a lot to what you will get out of this book!

An index and links to all the bonus content in this book can be found at: http://prosoundusa.com/HoldTheCheese

This book is meant to be a tool you can use to make a difference in your own business. At the end of the book, you will find a Caller Experience Checklist. Use this checklist to evaluate your own Caller Experience...what it's like for customers to call your business. Ask your employees what changes they would like to see. And don't be afraid to test. You cannot manage what you are unwilling to measure!

Praise for *Hold the Cheese!*

In a marketing world mesmerized by the latest and greatest gadgets and tactics, marketers often forget to tidy up the little things that are staring them smack-dab in the face ... critical areas of marketing like improving the caller's experience.
But not Chester Hull. His book, *Hold the Cheese!*, gets back to brass tacks and gives you a blueprint to transform your caller's experience — which is guaranteed to move your company's sales curve upward.
- Tom Wanek, author of *Currencies That Buy Credibility*

Chester Hull has created a phone guidebook for the modern age of communication. This book is full of practical advice for transforming your customer's phone experience from aggravating to downright fulfilling. And Chester goes much deeper than that…into the nooks and crannies of how the brain works, the psychology of it all and how it's all connected.
 If all you do is go through the Caller Experience Checklist, you will be providing your customers with a much-improved experience!
- Dave Young, marketing and customer experience consultant with *Wizard of Ads®*. Author of *Why We Blog*.

Everything customers feel on the phone is intangible, yet very real to them. When was the last time you reviewed your company's caller experience? Really reviewed it? Chester says what needs to be said. Don't skip this quick read.
- Paul Boomer, International Digital Marketing Strategist, Speaker and Consultant

Hold the Cheese is a great read for anyone in business...from front-line employees to C-level executives. It's easy and engaging, but all the while, challenging. You can't help but put your business under the microscope of *"Cheese"* to see how you stack up in light of what should be common sense. The use of QR codes and links throughout the book turn this into a great multi-media experience.
It's obvious that Chester has a passion for great customer experiences, and he wants you to also...so break off a hunk of cheese!
-Vince Koegle, Chairman, *On Hold Messaging Association*

Terrific information and an easy-to-read style!
In Hold the Cheese, Chester Hull reminds us that common sense must be exercised if we're to keep it common. Every one of these tips should be daily practice...Hold the Cheese challenges us: if we want to keep our customers front and center, we must remember the human basics.
- Bruce Balentine, author of *How to Build a Speech Recognition Application* and *It's Better to Be a Good Machine than a Bad Person.*

Contents

Introduction

How many times have you called a company and been frustrated by how its customer service representative handled your call? We've all experienced receptionists who make you wish you hadn't called, automated systems that feel like their only purpose is to overwhelm you with options, and voice-enabled systems that refuse to understand a word you say!

Did you know that 80 percent of companies think they are doing a great job at providing customer service? But their customers say only 8 percent are really delivering![1]

This book will help you understand what frustrates your callers, what your customers want, and how to deliver it. It's about making it easier to do business with you.

If someone gave you this book to read, it may be because they are trying to ask you to take a look at (or a listen to!) your own Caller Experience. Will you use the tools and information in this book to make a difference? I hope you do!

Here's to better Caller Experiences everywhere!

---

[1] http://www.bain.com/publications/articles/closing-the-delivery-gap-newsletter.aspx

Chapter 1
Sound On

Sound Branding

"A talking shark?"

"Yes, we'd like to give your shark mascot a voice for your On-Hold message. You already use the shark for your website, and you even have a full-size shark costume that represents you at community events and stuff. We love that, and we'd just like to bring that mascot to your callers by giving him a voice."

"But what does a shark sound like?" (Laughing now)

"Leave that to us...we'll dig into it."

"Okay, that sounds interesting. I'll look forward to hearing what you come up with!"

And with that, Gil the Shark found his voice for Big Surf Waterpark. A slightly sophisticated, experienced shark. Friendly and approachable, with a clear Australian accent:

http://prosoundusa.com/BigSurf

And now the callers could experience the same fun connection with Gil that you get when you visit the water park or you meet Gil around the community.

The phone is unique in that all the available sensory stimuli are compressed into one: Sound. How you sound becomes critical for influencing the caller in a positive way.

An Audio Brand denotes your company. It can be subtle and simple, or it can be loud and proud. But it is created to connect with your customers through the powerful medium of sound. An Audio Brand triggers connections to your callers' experiences with your company.

You may be thinking that your business or your brand doesn't really have a sound. That there doesn't need to be consistency for something you haven't got! But think about what you represent to customers when they walk into your place of business. There is sight. There is smell. There is touch. In some cases, there is taste. And there is sound. The complete sensory picture. For better or for worse, you have a few moments to draw that customer in, or to send him or her running to the door, never to return!

What is Audio Branding?

The Audio Branding Academy defines Audio Branding this way:

Audio Branding describes the process of brand development and brand management by use of acoustic elements within the framework of brand communication.

It is part of multi-sensory brand communication and holistic corporate design. Audio branding aims at building solidly a brand sound that represents the identity and values of a brand in a distinctive manner. The audio logo, brand music, or the brand voice are characteristic elements of audio branding.

This Audio Branding needs to be designed for any space where your customer hears from you.

When your customer walks into your business, what music does he or she hear? What sounds in general? Are those sounds consistent with your business' image?

When customers call your business, what do they hear? Is your phone system's recorded voice the same voice throughout? Or is it the voice of the receptionist who used to work for you, but has been gone for a year?

When that caller is On-Hold...can he still identify that it's the same company?

Margarita Bochmann, from Audi AG puts it this way:

"Concerning the effect on the emotional level and the communication of the brand image, sound is more efficient than visual elements. By using acoustic touch points like music on-hold, phone mailboxes, and the company's website, it is also possible for small and medium sized companies to do audio branding in a reasonable way."

Designing and implementing an "Audio Brand" is a critical piece of your overall Customer Experience.

Katz Creative created a very compelling presentation called the Power of Sound.

In it, Julian Treasure, author of *Sound Business*, says:

> *"Sight and hearing must be considered the twin major senses for two reasons. First, they can both carry specific messages: we can say exactly what we want in either vision or sound. Second, sight and hearing can both be broadcast, and they are therefore the only two mass communication senses. So far, nobody has found a way of broadcasting smells or tastes."*

In 1999, three scientists got together to study the influence of sound on product sales. Over a two-week period, French and German music was played on alternate days at an in-store display of French and German wines. French music led to French wines outselling German ones, whereas German music led to the opposite effect on sales.

Obviously, sound plays a critical role in the emotional connection a customer makes to your product or company.

Sound is Engineered

"Sonic branding is about getting something that sticks in someone's head and is not going away, even if you're not watching or not paying attention, you hear that sound and you know it." — Alex Moulton, Creative Director at Expansion Team

Did you know that Mercedes employs twelve engineers who are dedicated to fine-tuning the sound of opening and closing doors? Mercedes really takes its sonic brand seriously!

The sound a can of Pringles potato chips makes when opened is engineered to make you associate the product with freshness.

Brands you know by sound

Branding by sound is not a new concept. You would probably be surprised by how many brands have been consistently paying attention to how they sound for many years! How many of these brands can you identify by their signature sounds?

www.prosoundusa.com/Brands

Are you paying attention to the sound of branding all around you?

Audio Branding is about much more than simply having your secretary record the new Auto-Attendant greeting.

Effective Audio Branding is engineered to complement and enhance your company's sensory touch points. Audio Branding is as important to your customer as your visual brand. How important is it to you?

Sign of a Great Caller Experience

One day I was driving home from a camping trip with my family, and I decided to come home without traveling on the Interstate highways.

It was a beautiful day, and as we drove through small-town USA, it struck me how a business' presentation to passersby was critical to its survival! If the business had a good sign, a clear presentation, and was the type of place I was interested in stopping, I would be a customer.

But poor signage, a bad presentation, or no clear idea of what I would find inside would cause me to keep on driving (maybe never to pass that way again!).

While this concept may seem obvious to you, there's a parallel here for your business.

You've run your ads on radio, TV, billboards, and the Internet. You've spruced up your front entrance to make it appealing and inviting. You've educated your staff on how to ask the right questions of customers, without being pushy. Now you're waiting for customers to come pouring in your door.

Have you overlooked anything? I think you'll be surprised!

Your Caller Experience is a critical link to convincing new customers they should buy from you, and reinforcing that message to existing customers.

And just like the road signs I was watching as I traveled through small towns, you have but a few seconds to make or break that experience over the phone. Callers will put up with bad experiences for only so long.

So what makes for a bad experience? Here are a few situations that result in customers not wanting to do business with you:

- Poor phone skills: Staff who do not properly answer the phone, and do not place an importance on handling the phone call with clarity and promptness.
- Silence On-Hold, or even music alone: Callers don't know whether they've been disconnected, or simply put on "forget."

You wouldn't have an empty showroom when your customers walk in...so don't have "empty" On-Hold time. Nobody likes it.

- Long waits: Being On-Hold at some point is a fact of life. But don't forget about your caller On-Hold. Try to get back to him or her as quickly as possible!
- Transferred to the wrong person: Make sure when you transfer a caller that you stay on the line to make sure the caller gets to the right person or department. Your caller will really appreciate it.

Whether callers have these unpleasant experiences is one of the many the things you can measure by using a Secret Caller service, where calls are made into a business to test how its phones are answered. It's amazing how just a few small things can make a huge difference in how customers experience your business.

Those few seconds over the phone are critical to whether a customer chooses to do business with you…or go on to your competition.

What do *your* phones say about your company?

Chapter 2
Fishing with Phone Lines

Your Phone as a Useful Tool

Your customers can't possibly know every service you offer, or every item you carry. And while there is no way you can communicate all of that in a phone call, or how you answer the phone (more on that later!), you can pique your caller's interest.

That's "pique," which Dictionary.com defines as "to excite curiosity or interest." Highlighting a product per week, or a unique service each month, is a great way to pique people's interest and create Top of Mind Awareness. Top of Mind Awareness (or TOMA) means that people think of you or your company first when they want to buy the product or service you offer.

Sure, some of those people have already known that you offer that service, or you have sold that item since the day your business started. For those people, it's simply a reminder for when they need you. But others may have had no idea you carried the item they want and have been trying to find (or buy from your competitor), and they would rather bring their business to you!

One of the questions you should ask as you design your On-Hold message is "What do I do that no one knows about?

What's the thing about my company that you wish people were more aware of?"

Most of the time, the customer has an answer on the tip of his tongue. I was recently interviewing an insurance client who told me he was suffering from this very problem. His clients used him for auto, home, and business insurance, and they were very happy with him. But most had no idea that he offered health insurance as well. As an agency devoted to business clients, health insurance is very high on the list of things with which he would like to help his clients.

A second thing he told us about was life insurance. People don't often want to think about buying life insurance. But one day he picked up the phone to talk to a current client who had his home and auto insurance with this company, and that client said he had heard about life insurance while he was On-Hold. After talking through the options, and what the client needed, that client purchased a life insurance policy. The premium from that one purchase covered the cost of the On-Hold message service for an entire year! Studies show that when an insurance client adds a life insurance policy to his existing home and auto policies, the likelihood that he will remain with that insurance company rises to 95 percent.

Here's a situation where a business can use its phone to pique its caller's interest. The phone becomes the perfect tool to educate customers about your company. In this case, my client was already providing insurance services to customers, with which they were happy. Now, the next time one of his clients calls in to check on his policy or to make a change, my client has the opportunity to let that caller know about the health or life insurance options available.

So what are the ways you can use your phone to reach callers with relevant information? Let's look at a couple of ways.

First, one way to reach people is by including the information in the Queue or Hold message. Rather than simply make your callers wait in silence, hear an annoying "beep-beep," or listen to generic music, you can use that time to educate and inform your callers about your products or services that they may have not been aware you offered. Just like in the example of the insurance company, this method can be a very smart way to reach potential clients.

Another way to reach people at their moment of purchase is to play a message after the initial ring. When your caller dials your number, rather than hearing a continuous "ring-ring," they can hear a message like: *"Connecting your call. The health of your staff is critical to your business success. Ask us about protecting your business from unexpected expenses with the proper health insurance coverage."*

This message plays while the call rings through to the agency. One of the keys to making this method work is to educate your employees so they are aware of what your callers will be hearing. Then your employees will be prepared to answer any questions the caller may have as soon as they answer the phone.

One thing you don't want to do is cram it all into your initial greeting. One national plumbing franchise has the unique selling proposition that if its employees are late for the set appointment, it will pay you $5 for every minute they are late. Kinda makes waiting around for the repairman a little more fun, eh?

As a national franchise, this company also has specific rules for how to answer the phone. Its current script goes something like: "It's a great day at XYZ Plumbing[2], where if there's any delay, it's you we pay! This is Chester; how may we save you time today?"

Wow! By the time you've heard that, you could have solved your problem! In an effort to hit all their high-points, they extend the greeting to the point of becoming annoying. (And imagine if you were the one who had to say that every time the phone rang!)

If you draw the caller in, you will have the opportunity to sell to him later, the opportunity to explain what makes you different, and why the caller should choose you. Pay very close attention to the words you use to answer the phone. But don't cram your entire business proposition into the initial greeting!

---

[2] Not this company's real name

Again, choose a service or a product to highlight each week. Inform your staff of the item or service, and make that part of your outgoing message, and your On-Hold message.

Chapter 3
Who Should Be Answering Your Phone?

Live Answer or Auto-Attendant?

Take control of your phone experience to elevate your company by knowing when to use an automated attendant.

Have you made the decision to use an auto-attendant? What went into that decision? Your company needs an edge, and how your phone is answered is a critical place to start.

Consider this real-life example: A company I recently worked with had a "live answer only" policy, thinking it was pleasing its callers. But with four salespeople answering calls, callers had only a 25 percent chance of their specific salesperson answering the call. If the salesperson the caller wants to talk to does not answer the phone, it means the customer may experience hold time, transferring, and maybe even voicemail hell! Without a dedicated receptionist, a caller's experience will be different every time. And that's a difficult environment for making your company stand out!

Here's where you gain an edge. This environment is perfect for implementing an auto-attendant solution. But give your callers control over where they go. Offer your salespeople's extensions right up front, so callers can reach them by name, extension, or option. This offering gives callers a precision experience because they reach exactly the right person 100 percent of the time.

A second benefit to your company is eliminating interruptions and distractions for your employees. Pugh Research says that every time a call takes your employee off task, it takes up to ten minutes for him to recover. Once the employee no longer has to handle calls for co-workers, he will stay much more focused on the task at hand.

Your competition has made a knee-jerk reaction to how its phone is answered. Now you can get a step ahead by extending your superior showroom experience over the phone to your valuable callers.

Rock your customer's world while controlling the interruptions for your staff!

Live or auto-attendant? Evaluate your inside environment to make that decision with confidence.

Chapter 4
Answering the Call

Stop Talking and Start Answering

Time and again I've called a company...a professional business, mind you, and the person on the other end picks up the phone, but she hasn't fully finished the conversation she was already having! Does she think I can't hear her? Does she think the phone only starts working AFTER she has said, "Hello"?

If you're in a conversation with someone, but you need to answer the phone, simply stop talking, quickly excuse yourself from the conversation, and answer the phone!

When I hear bits and pieces of your conversation as you pick up the phone, it makes me, the caller, feel less important. It amplifies that I'm barging in on whatever you were doing. And sometimes, it reaches the level where I don't know whether you're talking to me or the other person!

So stop your previous conversation before you answer my call!

Answer with a Smile

The best way to convey cheerfulness on the phone is to be excited about answering it! When I was a kid, every phone call was an event. My sister and I raced each other to the nearest phone, knocking down tables, leaping over toys, and diving or sometimes sliding around the corner...arms reaching to grab the phone. And yet, as out of breath as we may have been, we would somehow be able to control the breathing, control the excitement of getting there first, and answer the phone with a clear "Hello?"...and a solid question mark on the end of the word.

Even when you don't feel especially happy, it's hard NOT to improve your mood by simply lifting up the corners of your mouth. Go ahead...try it now! Now with a great big smile on your face, try to be angry! Go ahead; I dare you! The reason smiling works is because the human body associates physical responses with associated emotion. So when you smile, it automatically lifts your emotions, in turn making you happier!

Remember this...happiness is frequently a choice. So make up your mind to be happy...BEFORE you pick up the phone...even if it's for the ninety-eighth time today!

Be Genuine

When you answer with genuineness, you make a quick human connection with the caller. This connection will make the caller feel more comfortable, especially if he is unsure of whom he needs to talk to, or what he should ask for.

Being genuine means concentrating on the present. What's important right now? Answering the phone...connecting with your caller. Make that personal connection.

Connect with Interest

Because the caller can't see you, it's even more important to convey the cues to him that you are glad he called, and you are ready to help him.

Answer with a question mark at the end of your greeting...your voice going up slightly at the end...inviting the caller to say the next thing. You can do that whether you say, "Hello?", "How may I help you?", or you answer with your name, as in "This is Chester?" We're going to look at how to choose what you say when you answer the phone in the next section. Just remember that you want to invite the caller to participate with you in the conversation. Make him or her feel welcome.

What to say when you do answer

Don't say your entire sales spiel.

A long greeting causes your caller to be uncomfortable, unsure whether you're quite finished, and even interrupt you before you finish! This situation makes the initial interaction an awkward one.

Remember the plumbing company from Chapter 2? When it's time to decide how to answer your phone, it can serve as an example for good...and for bad. You should have scripts for your front line people. How they answer the phone is critical to how people perceive your business, so you don't want to leave that up to chance.

But don't put your entire sales spiel into that script...no matter how tempting that may be! Your frontline phone people will be dealing with a large number of calls, and it is more customer-friendly to limit the greeting. Sure, if you've got some major promotion that will affect a lot of people, then let them know. But keep it brief...no more than a few words.

Confirm the company name, and provide your first name

Here's an example: *"Charter Insurance. This is Julie."* This greeting confirms for the caller that he reached the right company (you'd be surprised how many people dial the wrong number!), and it gives your name as an invitation for the caller to use it to springboard into the conversation. You have now become the "voice" of the company. And with that power comes a responsibility to provide a great customer experience.

Ask how you may direct the person's call, unless you can answer his or her questions

One thing a lot of companies do that frustrates callers is asking, "How may I help you?" when really what they mean is, "How may I direct your call?" Those greetings give two entirely different meanings to the caller.

The first says: *"I've reached someone who can bridge between myself and this company, probably looking into any records the company has about me or my purchase, and can probably make a decision regarding my concern."* If that's truly the case with whomever answers the phone at your business, then including, "How may I help you?" in your script is great.

However, more often than not, when we hear that question, all the person is really authorized to do is transfer your call to someone else who does in fact have the ability to find you in her computer. Do you see the difference? When you hear someone answer with, *"How may I direct your call?"* you instantly know that this person won't be the one helping you solve your problem, or answering your question, but she very likely will be a big help in getting you to the right person. The more obscure your question, the more you need this person's help and knowledge of the inner workings of the company in order to transfer you to the right person. *"How may I help you?"*, if spoken by someone who really just wants to transfer the call, will cause customer frustration!

So pay attention to these minor word differences when crafting your phone answering script...they can make a big impact on the service you deliver over the phone.

Keep a Notepad Handy

Always keep a notepad and pen handy near your phone. When you use it every call, you'll begin capturing really important information. Start with the name of the caller as soon as he gives it. This way you can use it during the conversation. Use it to refer back to the call, or when transferring the call to someone else.

If you use a flip-notebook, you'll easily be able to go back and find a name, phone number, or detail that you need later.

One of the things that is really neat about Click and Clack, the Car Talk Guys, is that they use the caller's name quite a bit, and they deal with a tremendous amount of information on each call! They don't just remember all that stuff...they're writing it down as the call happens!

Start doing that yourself and you'll sound like a hero to your callers!

Use an Auto-Attendant as a Backup

One way to use effectively both a live answer, and an auto-attendant system, is to use the Auto-Attendant as a backup. Rather than letting the phone ring when your normal receptionist is busy, hoping that someone else will pick up the phone, direct it to your Auto-Attendant. The really beautiful thing is that most phone systems include a basic Auto-Attendant in them, so it's simply a matter of turning it on or setting it up.

Here's a significant advantage: your receptionist knows how to direct callers efficiently to the correct places. If that person is busy, and you allow the phone to ring to whomever might answer, not only will you take someone off-task, but that person isn't used to answering the phone. The greeting that person uses, and her familiarity (or lack of) with routing calls could provide a negative caller experience.

Using an Auto-Attendant as a backup, you get the advantage of a live person answering the phone, while still covering that person when call volume is too much for her to handle, or she is simply tied up with another caller.

Using the Auto-Attendant also gives you the opportunity to highlight a special or promotion that the customer may not have known about. Pizza shops use this opportunity quite a bit to play their weekly special to callers BEFORE they answer the phone live to take their order. Those pizza shops that take advantage of this tool experience a tremendous uplift in advertised items, like extra garlic bread, drinks, and desserts.

The Phone or a Live Person?

How do decide whom to help?

How many times has this happened to you? Your front door opens, and in walks a new customer. At the same moment, the phone begins to ring. In a lot of small businesses, answering the phone and helping the walk-in customer both fall to the same person. Do you let the phone ring? Or do you hold up your hand to the customer, in the unspoken language of "wait," and answer the phone? Which customer is more important?

Making _both_ feel important

That's right...both, and it's your job to make both _feel_ important. So how do you do that? First of all, have a backup plan for you phones. It doesn't matter if it's a customer walking in the door, or one more line ringing that you can't answer, you need to have a backup plan for your phones. Tip: A busy signal isn't a backup plan! If you've chosen to live answer every call...if that's your effort, and you've determined that is the best approach, it still will be a good idea to have a well-designed Auto-Attendant as a backup plan. At some point you _will_ need it.

The easiest thing is to let the phone ring to your backup plan while you help the walk-in customer. The live person can see your actions; the caller can't. The caller doesn't know whether or not you are deferring her. The walk-in customer does. So help the walk-in customer. Let the call go to your backup plan.

That doesn't just mean letting the call go to your normal voicemail that says, "Sorry. We're closed." If your Auto-

Attendant is a backup for a primary live answer, you can design it to help the customer. Here are some tips to include in the greeting:

- Let the caller know your staff is busy.
- Give the caller options to reach people or departments for which he may be calling. You may not need to handle his call at all!
- Provide a voicemail option if the caller really would rather leave a message. But give him some kind of promised follow-up time for his message. ("We promise to call you back within the next two hours.")
- Ask the caller to hold (and if your system supports it, give him the option to wait in queue). If your phone system doesn't support a caller waiting in queue, you could answer the phone and ask him to hold. But make sure you wait for the answer! The caller may just need to transfer to another person, so you can quickly handle that for him without neglecting the walk-in customer. It really is a juggling act!

Be confident of your backup plan

Test your backup plan. Make sure that if you're on the phone, calls will be handled properly. Nothing is worse than "thinking" it works, when it really doesn't. Or it sounds poor. Or it doesn't provide the options you thought it did. Test your backup plan. It's not a "plan" unless it's been tested!

Chapter 5
Hand It Over

Let Callers Know They Are Going to be Transferred

Before you simply press the transfer button, make sure your caller knows that you're going to transfer him. Give him enough time to interject in case he only needs to ask a simple question or he would rather call back instead of being transferred. A lot of times, you may be able to answer a quick question, without having to transfer the caller to someone else. Regardless, don't simply press the transfer button as soon as the caller has asked to be transferred. You can reply with a simple, "I'll transfer you now" to help the caller.

Always Do an Assisted Transfer

I once called the credit card company to ask for a credit increase on my business credit card. The IVR (Interactive Voice Response) system easily walked me through the process of entering my account information, entering the amount of credit I was requesting, and entering income details. It then proceeded to ask me to wait while it transferred me to a representative.

I expected the representative to pick up right where the system left off, to complete the application, and to provide my results.

Boy was I disappointed in the caller experience! The phone system didn't hand off any of my information. The representative answered the call as if I had just called in, and he had no idea that I was in the middle of a credit increase request. In fact, as I explained to him the process I had been walked through by the IVR, he sounded slightly amazed, as if he didn't realize his phone system did that!

As I explained my story, he offered to put me through to the "Credit Increase Department," which sounded promising to me.

The representative who answered the phone continued my disappointment with the company. She did not know my name, (which I had by now given twice), she did not know what I was calling about (which I had now given twice), and she did not have my account information (which I had now given...yep, you guessed it...two times!)

She offered to submit a request for me, and I proceeded to give her all my information (again).

I then asked about the company's sixty day policy. You see, this credit card company has a policy that it will not raise a credit limit within sixty days of opening the account.

Now, this situation wouldn't normally be a problem, except that my company had just moved from a credit card with one bank to this new card at a new bank. The new bank, in its infinite wisdom, decided that our business only needed a credit line that was 15 percent of our old card.

I asked whether there was someone I could speak to about authorizing an increase. I was told, "No, there isn't, not within sixty days."

I explained how this situation was making it quite difficult to run a small business. This company markets itself as the Small Business Solution…the one thing you need if you're a small business. But then it made it incredibly difficult to do business with its company.

The representative did tell me that the soonest the company could offer an increase would be the 15th of December (which, ironically, was *less* than sixty days after the account was opened!), and suggested I call back then.

So how could this company have handled this situation better? Let's count the ways:

- The IVR system could include a message about the sixty day policy.

- The IVR could complete the process without the hand-off to a representative

- The IVR could display my information to the rep, so he would be instantly up to speed on what my call was all about.

- The IVR could have transferred me directly to the Credit Increase Department since it already knew that's what I wanted.

- The rep who did transfer me to the Credit Increase Department could have made an Assisted Transfer, passing along my story (and my name and account information) to the next representative.

- With a company policy in place that shackles her hands, this representative wasn't going to be able to change a lot for me. However, rather than ask me to call back, she could offer to be proactive, take my information, and submit the request on the 15th, rather than make me start the process over again.

- The representative also could offer to contact me with the results or any questions at that time.

Any of these things would be an improvement on how this company handled my call. This incident may have cost them having my company as a client, and I know I'm not the only one who has had this experience!

So why should you care about my experience with some unnamed credit card bank?

Hundreds or thousands of customers and prospects are calling your business every week. Have you thought about what their caller experience is like and how you can improve it?

Just a few simple changes like these can make a world of difference in how your customers feel about your business. Don't make it difficult to do business with you!

Pass along as Much Information as Possible

If you are transferring someone, pass along as much information as possible. The person's name, why he is calling, anything you've done so far to try to resolve the situation or answer the question, and even the caller's mood.

If you're on the receiving end of a transfer, let the caller know you have his information. You can do so simply by greeting him with his name, and then saying, "Joan gave me your information, and it looks like you need some help with resetting your debit card pin?" That's both a summary, as well as a question to confirm that you understand why the person is calling.

Here is something else interesting about an assisted transfer. Lots of times, I hear a person answer the ringing phone, begin the transfer, and then yell across the room to let the called party know who is calling him! An assisted transfer would have allowed the person to use the phone as an intercom, delivering the information without having to yell!

Make Sure the Transfer Goes Through

When you do a transfer, make sure it goes through before you hang up. I've been bounced around companies multiple times because someone simply answered the phone, transferred me into oblivion, and moved on to the next caller. It only takes a moment to make sure the person you are transferring the caller *to* is the correct person, and whether he is available, or if you can connect the caller to him in some other way.

Chapter 6
Calming the Waters

At one time or another, we all are going to have to answer the phone to talk with an angry or upset caller. When that situation happens, here are a few things to remember.

Don't React in Frustration

If you match the caller's anger or upset feelings in your response to him, the call, and the relationship, will quickly melt into a puddle of irreplaceable hard feelings. So the first thing to do is...to NOT do! Don't react with frustration; don't respond in anger, and don't even make a smart comment. The best thing to do is to stay calm.

Empathize with the Caller

Most of the time, if you can empathize with the caller, you will gain his ear, and calm him down at the same time. Empathy is understanding or entering into another's feelings. Convey that you understand why the caller might be upset, and that it's not an unreasonable reaction (even if it's not the most productive reaction!). Seeing the situation from the caller's perspective is the first thing the caller really wants you to do.

Take Some Blame for the Company

I recently had an excellent example of an employee taking the blame for the company when I called Starbucks. I had purchased a coffee cup, and used it once, and the second time I went to use it, my coffee poured out all around the lid! As coffee ran down my chin and on my shirt, I couldn't believe what was happening! When I took off the cup's lid, I saw right away that the cup had been cracked, all around the top, and there was no way it could be fixed. I called Starbucks to ask what it suggested I do about this situation since I suspected that the first time I used the cup, a barista had dropped it, and I felt that could have caused the cracking.

When I spoke with the Starbucks representative, the first thing he did was take full responsibility for the incident. No questions asked. There was never any implication that it might have been my fault, and never any hedging on the fact that the company was going to take care of me. Right away, he asked whether I could send him the receipt for the cup so he could give me a refund. Unfortunately, I didn't have the receipt anymore, so he asked what I had paid for the cup. I told him it was ten or eleven dollars to the best of my memory. He let me know that without the receipt, he couldn't issue an exact refund, but that he would be happy to send me a $10 gift card if that were acceptable to me. He also took careful notes of the cup type, and let me know that the company tracks incidents with its cups, so it can improve on them.

Then, in a move that sealed my feelings about Starbucks, he said, "Now, you mentioned that it spilled on your shirt. Is there anything we need to do to clean or replace your shirt?" Do you see how taking the blame for the incident led him to going beyond what I felt was even necessary in order to resolve my situation? But if he had been hedging up front, and even grudgingly offered a refund, I wouldn't have felt nearly as good about the company as I do now! (And sharing this story with you is free press for Starbucks!)

By taking the blame for the company, the employee allowed for there to be only a very small step between solving my complaint, and making me a fan of Starbucks for life!

Empower Your Customer Service People

I'm a huge fan of empowering your front line people to do what they need to do in order to make your customers happy. I'm constantly baffled at companies that give their Customer Service Reps the power to make very attractive offers to potential or former customers, but if I, as an existing customer, am unhappy or upset, there is virtually nothing they can offer to keep me as a customer.

Ann Brady[3] talks about an experience she and her husband had with their satellite dish company. After more than four years as a loyal, paying customer, they noticed a problem

---

[3] Ann Brady - http://www.customerservicemanager.com/empowering-customer-service-vital.htm

with the reception. When they asked to have someone come take a look at it, they were told it would be $100. That is the only option customer service was empowered to offer. When Ann informed the customer service rep that she could get brand new satellite equipment for free from the company's competitor, she was told to go ahead and switch, which Ann and her husband did. After they switched, the first company called to ask why they left, so Ann told them the story. The employee agreed that "After four years, we should have fixed it for free." Too late. Ann had signed a new one-year agreement and couldn't be happier with their new, free, digital video recorder.

Examples like these are not at all uncommon in the customer service world. Give your customer service people...your frontline customer contact points...the power to solve customers' problems—to do whatever it takes (within reason) to make your customers happy.

Here are some tips for empowering your customer service department:

1.) Depending on the nature of the complaint, arm your customer service employees with the ability to offer incentives to unhappy customers to encourage them not to leave.

For example, if you normally charge for a service call, but you're facing the prospect of losing a ten-year customer, allow the customer service representative to offer half off.

2.) If your company screwed up, and your customer calls you on it, allow your customer service people to admit that a mistake was made, apologize, and offer something to make up for it, perhaps a free month of service, or a coupon for a discount on a future order.

Nothing is more aggravating than having someone apologize without admitting any wrongdoing (i.e. "I'm sorry you feel that way," or "I'm sorry you're upset about that.") Teach your people to say, "I'm sorry; we were wrong. What can we do to make it up to you?" While the customer isn't "always right," reacting this way can go a long ways toward keeping a customer.

3.) Toss the scripts. Giving customer service people lists of things to say to unhappy customers turns your people into nothing more than robots. With today's voice recognition technology, you may as well use an automated response system.

Train your customer service people on how to act like human beings. Provide them with the kind of conflict-resolution training they need to turn unhappy customers into people who at least believe your company cares about their problems and wants to help them.

4.) Offer incentives to customer service people who retain unhappy customers.

For example, record your calls, and once a month give an award to the customer service representative who does the best job turning angry customers into happy ones.

5.) Don't wait for the customer to insist on speaking to a manager. If the customer service representative's authority to offer a solution is not enough to retain the customer, it should be standard procedure for the representative to request time to consult a supervisor and possibly bring him or her into the discussion.

Chapter 7
How to Think Like a Caller

Inside the Caller's Head

It's hard to read the label from inside the bottle. "Huh?" you say. Here is what I mean: What you think is your "inside reality"—the customer experience inside your doors—is only what your customer says it is. Nothing more. And thankfully, nothing less. That also means you have the opportunity to surprise and delight your customer with unexpected service.

A while back, I ended up owning two identical, brand new iPads. Well, when I found out I wouldn't have to pay a restocking fee to Apple to return one of them, I decided to send one back. It was only *after* I decided to return one that I found out Apple not only would not charge a restocking fee, but they would send me a prepaid return shipping label, and the return wouldn't cost me a thing. As in free! I was delighted.

And the reason I was delighted (aside from saving the money, of course) is because it was unexpected. Nowhere does Apple advertise "Free return shipping…you can send it back, and not pay a dime!" It's just something Apple does, and it makes me like doing business with them.

So what do you do to delight your customers? What are the little…or big…things you could do to surprise and delight your existing customers? Strengthening the bond with your existing customer base is one of the best ways to increase your revenue.

So why is it that it often goes the other way? You woo customers in with fantastic ads and heartfelt promises, but then once they're "in the fold," they are no longer on the "To Be Delighted" list?

So here's a way to have some fun, and maybe discover some ways to delight more customers:

- Get out of the office…business…or whatever work environment you are in. That's right, go ahead.

- Grab a cup of your favorite beverage, and contemplate your business category:

  - Are there any preconceived notions or misconceptions that prevent more people from coming to your business, or buying what you sell?

  - What mistakes do some competitors make? That is, how could they create a more fulfilling customer experience?

- Now, call your business, and ask for directions to your store. Pay attention to what this experience sounds like… how the phone is answered…what you hear as a customer.

- Walk into your business and buy something. Was it easy? Did you enjoy the experience? What was the environment like?

Sometimes it takes getting out of the familiar to see things from another perspective. And even then it's hard! You might be surprised at the view from outside the bottle!

Give Callers Personal Value

The party line is dead.

It's over.

Replaced by the sophistication of electronics. (That is, unless you live in one of the eighty-one cabins in Big Santa Anita Canyon high above L.A.[4])

Ahhhh, the steamroller of progress. A very good thing this time.

The party line's completely non-private service made eavesdropping opportunities abound. If another caller were on the line when you needed to make a call…too bad…you were waiting.

But when it comes to business, have you realized that the party line is dead? No longer do multiple people share a phone call to your company.

---

[4] http://en.wikipedia.org/wiki/Party_line_(telephony)

It's a direct, one-to-one relationship. Have you customized your On-Hold message to reflect that reality?

Talk to that one caller in his or her language.

"Well, how?" you say. "How can I have a customized On-Hold message? Lots of people call me!"

Right, but have you considered who those "lots of people" really are?

Mike Wittenstein, Chief Experience Officer at Storyminers, says the most important factor for delivering a great customer experience is to know your customer. Personally. [5] That personal knowledge allows you to understand how your product, service, or company fits into the customer's life—what it is that makes him or her value your product.

Rather than build the Caller Experience with your *entire* customer list in view, pick one, and design it for that customer. Choose a customer you know personally, and build your message around how your product or service improved that customer's life. Tell a story, with your customer as the star.

Sure, other callers will hear that. And when it doesn't fit their exact situations, they'll think, "Wow, if this company is 'all that' for that customer, it can probably solve my problem as well!"

---

[5] http://rbd.doingbusiness.ro/ro/opinii/17/improve-customer-experience-the-perfect-recipe-for-hard-times

Applying this tactic to other areas of your Caller Experience is even more straightforward. Here's a great example from DSW Shoes:

http://prosoundusa.com/OneToOne

You see, if you want to connect with an individual caller, you have to talk to them like an individual!

"Don't Put Me On-Hold!"

How often have you heard, "Don't put me On-Hold!" I'll bet you've thought that a few times yourself!

Being On-Hold is often a frustrating experience. But let's break it down to examine why it's frustrating.

Taking your time

Number one, it's taking up your time. Time that could be spent doing other things. And companies that have long hold times (we're talking more than five minutes or so), really need to reevaluate their staffing or procedures for handling calls.

Silence

Ah…the dreaded silence. Have I been disconnected? Am I being transferred? Did I just get put into the phone system's Black Hole? (Most phone systems have one of those — you knew that, right? Somewhere that callers go, never to be heard from again!) As a business, putting your callers On-Hold to silence is one of the worst things you can do to hurt your Caller Experience. It's like asking people to stand in line with a blindfold on. They're just not going to stick around! But give them something relevant and interesting to listen to while they're On-Hold, and the wait time will seem very much diminished!

It's all about me

If you do have an On-Hold message…congratulations on "getting it." Now, what does it say? You see, callers want to hear about themselves. They want to hear how your service or products are going to make their lives better…how they are going to help them and change their lives for the better. They don't want to hear a message that is all about you — all about how long you've been in business or how great you or your products are. This kind of message comes across the phone lines as "blah, blah, blah." But tell a story, make the caller the star, and you'll experience a much happier customer when you pick up the phone!

Changing the message

One of the keys to having a great caller experience is to keep the message current and up-to-date. So how do you do that? How do you know when to change it, how often to change it, and what to change? That depends on a number of factors. What is the profile of your caller? In other words, does he call in regularly, once a week, month, or year? Or does he interact with you heavily for a week, then not at all for a couple of months? How long is he On-Hold? What are the top three or four things callers ask about when they call in? Is there information that would really be helpful for them to hear? These are some of the questions that you need to consider as you walk through the process of creating a complete On-Hold program.

It's not just as simple as slapping a message on your phones, and checking that off the To-Do list. If you really want a powerful Caller Experience, it takes understanding your business, understanding your caller, and understanding how people think.

Chapter 8
Hold the Cheese!

Most On-Hold messages are cheesy. Cheesy because they talk about things that callers don't care about, in a way that doesn't make callers want to listen. For example, reminding you that "Your call is important to us" and to "Please continue to hold" simply frustrates your caller even more! Cheesy because someone simply didn't take the time to ask, "Will our callers think this sound cheesy?"

Most On-Hold experiences are not fun and engaging. Most callers would ask not to be put On-Hold…and some will demand not to be!

But with a little effort and thought, you can create an On-Hold experience that has callers asking to be put back On-Hold!

Do You Need an On-Hold Message?

One question I get asked in the On-Hold message consultations my company offers is whether or not a company can benefit from a custom On-Hold message.

So how will you, the busy business owner, know when an investment to reach your callers while On-Hold will return good results?

How many calls do you receive?

Over the course of a day, a week, or even a month…how many calls does your business receive? Have you ever thought about counting them? Have you ever tried?

You could get your receptionist or employees just to make a quick tally whenever they answer the calls. It might not be the most technologically advanced method, but it will give you a better understanding of how many calls you do receive!

How long are callers On-Hold?

I talk with some companies who tell me, "We don't put people On-Hold," but willing it not to happen doesn't mean it never does.

Being On-Hold is a fact of life for most businesses. But On-Hold time really falls into two categories:

1. Long hold times…like call centers, tech support, and customer service. These are hold times counted in tens of minutes. (I know…I was On-Hold with American Express for forty-two minutes!)

2. Short hold times…these are hold times that we often don't think about. Being transferred to another person, sent to voicemail, or waiting while someone looks up our order. These hold times are usually measured in seconds. You may be On-Hold for ten seconds while going to voicemail, thirty seconds while being transferred to the person with whom you would

like to speak, or for a minute or two while someone looks up your order or checks the stock of an item.

These two very different categories require different approaches. But for category #2, which most small businesses fall into, optimizing that On-Hold time can bring great value to the caller.

So how do you measure it?

Spend two days asking your staff to track how many calls go On-Hold or are transferred. Again, a simple tally will work. Monitoring a few of those calls will give you a great idea of how long the average hold time is at your company.

With that information, you can begin to measure the value that a custom On-Hold message can bring to your company.

And if your business really is one of those that doesn't put people On-Hold, you'll find that out as well.

Quantifying the Caller Experience will give you a clearer picture of the areas where your Caller Experience can improve to maximize customer service.

Remember, you can't improve what you don't measure!

On-Hold Options

This TED video from Julian Treasure has a lot to teach about the use of sound in business. Take a moment to watch it, and then I'll point out a few ways you can make the most of this information.

http://prosoundusa.com/Sound

First, you may have noticed some pretty big numbers....a drop of 66 percent in productivity in open-plan office environments and a sales drop of up to 28 percent in a retail environment when inappropriate sound is present.

I especially liked his observation that we, "...move away from unpleasant sound and toward comfortable sounds."

Telephone Sound is one of eight types of commercial sound that Treasure talks about. If you haven't thought about the rest of your soundscape, your phone sound signature is a good place to start. A Caller Experience expert can help craft your phone sound to be a reflection of your business goals. You can go from there into more purposeful and directed tactics for every other element of sound in the business.

If you already have a unique soundscape in your advertising, in-store experience, products and services, you've made that expert's job easier, but no less urgent.

Crafting and producing an On-Hold message is not good territory for Do-It-Yourself business marketers. As a business owner, you're likely only to mention information that's important to *you*, while failing to take a customer-centric view. You risk falling into instruction mode instead of taking an informative and (if appropriate) entertaining strategy.

But not all On-Hold message companies are created equal. Here are some of the pitfalls to watch out for from any On-Hold provider:

- They offer "canned," pre-produced, or fill-in-the-blank messages.
- They expect the business owner to write the scripts.
- They leave it up to you to remember to make changes to your message throughout the year.
- They make no attempt to customize your message to match the sound signature of your business and other marketing efforts.
- They provide equipment that doesn't allow instant updates, flexible scheduling, and constant monitoring.

A great On-Hold message provider will:

- Thoroughly uncover the key values of the business.
- Dig deep enough to find the important facts for the message.

- Provide turn-key support and quick response for updating messages.
- Provide advanced playback equipment.
- Monitor your system's actual playback on a regular basis.

I like Treasure's first three golden rules of commercial sound:

1. Make it congruent (with the core values and other sound elements of the business).
2. Make it appropriate (to the intended listeners).
3. Make it valuable (by offering more than a caller expected to hear).

So, what's holding you back?

If you're abusing your customers by delivering a bad phone experience, it is one of the easiest marketing touch points to fix.

If you're not sure what kind of experience you're delivering, get it evaluated.

If you currently offer flat, dead silence, that's the best place to start.

Anatomy of an On-Hold Message

I was recently placed On-Hold at a financial institution, and heard this On-Hold message:

http://prosoundusa.com/OnHoldAnatomy

I was struck by a couple of things, and since Prosound did not produce this On-Hold message, I'm going to break it down for you here.

First of all, it's not just a "thank you for holding" message. There's more information in there to let me know I've called a financial institution.

It has holiday closings listed, which is fantastic! (It's always good to communicate closings and hour changes with your customers as much as possible!)

There are tips for online shopping security, as well as shopping in the "real" world.

And there's even a reminder to change your clock back to Standard Time on Sunday, November 7th.

So, what's missing?

Nowhere…not once…ever…is the name of the financial institution listed. Go back and listen again, if you didn't catch it. It's all right; I'll wait.

"So what's the big deal?" you might ask.

Here's the thing:

This strategy is quite brilliant actually—but only for the On-Hold message production company. It has created a set of messages that is recorded once, and sold over and over again to financial institutions nationwide.

The strategy is not so brilliant for the bank that's using it, and here's why:

* It doesn't reinforce the name of the bank to each and every customer.

* It doesn't help strengthen the bank's other marketing and branding efforts outside the bank, like it could if it were part of those efforts.

* It lacks a distinct relevance that only a unique On-Hold message can provide. Relevance is created by connecting with the perspective of the listener. The more specific you can be in your messaging, the more believable your message will be.

Every business has a story to tell.

Telling the story that is uniquely yours will create stronger relationships with your clients and prospects, making it a much harder choice for them to leave you, or to choose your competition.

I admit that finding your unique story is more difficult than simply selecting a few pseudo-customized-for-your-industry messages. But your customers and callers will thank you.

Keep these things in mind as you approve your ad copy…whatever medium it's in:

- Ads that fail in one medium will usually fail in others.

- The medium is not the message; the message is the message.

- And the message is what matters most[6].

---

[6] http://www.entrepreneur.com/advertising/adcolumnistroyhwilliams/article178044.html

Meet Jack

When First National Bank of the South adopted Jack the Dog as their new mascot, they also gained a unique marketing opportunity. No other bank could use the same mascot to differentiate themselves to customers. And in the world of banking, where little seems to stand out from one bank to the next, Jack the Dog could help First National Bank of the South stand out. Here is an example of an On-Hold message that is unique, customized for one specific bank, and unusable by any competitor:

http://prosoundusa.com/MeetJack

It connects deeply with listeners because it's a continuation of the branding that this bank is doing on its website. And it's relevant to the caller because it invites him or her into the story ("Meet Jack").

Speak to the Felt Need

For the 2011 Super Bowl, Old Spice started a series of fantastic ads that got a lot of media attention.

Here is what was so amusing to me about their ads:

You have no idea what Isaiah Mustafa smells like in that commercial!

I was kind of surprised that this didn't jump out at me sooner. Old Spice did an excellent job of triggering one sense (your sense of smell)…without even using scent! It *only* used visual and aural senses to sell a smell.

Whoa! That's some powerful engagement there! And I've seen that ad countless times, without realizing what was happening! (It also helps that I know what Old Spice body wash smells like!)

From the ad: "If he stopped using lady-scented body wash, and switched to Old Spice, he could smell like he's me."

Go back and read that again.

Watch the video if you want; I'll wait.

http://prosoundusa.com/OldSpice

Now, what's the point, and why would I want to make it here?

The point is that you don't have to *use* all five senses to engage fully your prospect's five senses.

Did you know the body needs "just" 100 million sensory receptors to experience the physical universe around you?

By contrast, your mental and emotional universe is so complex that your brain requires 10,000 billion synapses to experience the world inside your head! (You don't have to take my word for it. Learn about the twelve languages of the mind.)

We are much more prepared to experience the world of imagination and dream than we are the physical world.

Words, sounds, images, and more are what transport us into those worlds. And you can use that same transport to take your customer there.

The Caller Experience a customer has when phoning your business sets that caller up for how he or she is going to experience your product or service. Are you providing a great experience?

Here are some complaints that businesses have gotten that have caused them to talk to us lately:

- "The voice just wasn't warm and fuzzy."
- "Your receptionist hung up on me in the middle of my saying goodbye!"
- "I hear our receptionist saying: 'I don't know… that's not my job,' rather than "I can find out and get back with you."

How your phone is answered gives people a glimpse inside your company. And just like Isaiah and Old Spice, they don't have to see with their physical eyes to imagine with their mind's eye!

Thinking about the possibilities? Think about this.

What does it sound like when you push that little red "Hold" button on your phone? Do your callers get dumped into a black cavern of silence, wandering around looking for daylight, sometimes for long periods of time?

Do they hear the same generic music your competitors have, with constant reminders to "Please stay on the line….please! We're begging you!"?

Or do you transport them to a magical place, where you engage their senses in a way that is interesting, fun, and still relevant to your business?

Just like what was done here, for Southern States? They wanted to highlight their chicken feed, and what better way than to…well, I'll let the chickens speak for themselves:

http://prosoundusa.com/talkingchickens

You can engage your customers' minds and draw them into your business, or you can leave them in silence to contemplate the myriad other thoughts they're faced with each day. Your choice…what does your phone sound like?

Move the Needle on the "Who Cares" Meter

You've just called the Wagon Yard, a furnishings and collectibles store in Texas. You're calling about the 54″ cherry roll-top computer desk you heard that it carried. That would look great in your office! And while you are transferred to the furniture department, you hear this:

http://prosoundusa.com/WagonYardOnHold

Now you're interested in more than just a roll-top desk! And why is that?

Because a compelling, relevant On-Hold message moves the "Who Cares" meter!

I'm sure you've heard or seen the opposite in an ad… maybe even today. "We've been in business since…." Really?

Who cares?

Now you're probably saying, "But Chester, I don't want to do business with a fresh, young, inexperienced company!" Really? Like Google? Facebook? Twitter? These are all companies that developed huge (did I say huge?) customer bases, and they weren't built around how long they had been in business.

Let's break this point down a little more. When a company leads with how long it has been in business, what is it really trying to say?

- Its experience makes it the expert.
- You will be able to count on warranty support.
- You won't be left "holding the bag" if something goes wrong.

I'm sure we could come up with a lot more things here.

Any one of those would be more compelling…more interesting to you and me as customers, than, "We've been in business since…"

Why is that? It's because of the difference between facts and emotion.

Facts say you've been in business for fifty years.

Emotions tell me that I want to buy from someone who is an expert.

Phrases like "family-owned," "superior service," and "exceptional value" don't create a strong emotional reason to do business with your company. Don't get me wrong; it's nice information. But it's not the "bottom-line food-truth"[7] about your business that is going to get your visitors salivating for what you have to offer.

---

[7] http://www.grokdotcom.com/messagemustbemeat.htm

Draw me into the world of emotions, and I am more likely to find interest in your product or service. And the best way to engage the emotional side of the brain is to tell a story.

Tell me a story…make me a star.

Tell your customer a story, with him as the star, and you will instantly engage his emotional power. (Take a moment to go back and read the first paragraph of this section again. Did you notice it was about you?)

When we tell stories, we engage the emotion rather than the intellect. Emotion and intellect are not connected! Intellectual ads are about inarguable facts. It's about "New!" (when it really *is* new!)

But emotional ads are about what the customer already knows or feels. They connect with what we already believe to be real, while adding a new perspective.

We do what feels right; then we use our intellectual logic to justify our emotional decision.

So the next time you're thinking about what callers hear while On-Hold, take out the intellect, and put in the emotion. It will make a powerful difference!

Don't Remind Them They Are On-Hold

Adam Alter has written an interesting article about the quirks in time perception[8] that we all share. Why does the first hour of a long flight seem *sooo* long, while the last several hours all cram together in your mind?

---

[8] http://www.psychologytoday.com/blog/alternative-truths/201004/quirks-in-time-perception

I'll bet you've had a similar experience in micro…the last time you called a company and were put On-Hold. With so many things that need to be done in our busy lives, no one wants to wait, and who can blame us?

Have you been in Best Buy and had to wait in line to check out? What do you do while you wait? You probably skim the end caps, but I'll bet you spend most of the wait watching the Best Buy TV program on one of the many screens the store has positioned in site. Why do they put those there?

Because when your mind is engaged, it doesn't think about the amount of time you've been waiting. It feels like only a few seconds, when really the store has been able to play four one-minute promos for you!

Now back to the On-Hold. If your business is putting people On-Hold and just having them listen to silence, you're actually extending the perceived wait time. How would you like it if Best Buy required you to put on a blindfold while you stood in line? Every second would feel like an hour until you could take that blindfold off!

But if you choose to engage your callers during those inevitable times they have to wait On-Hold, then the amount of time they perceive they are waiting will be quite a bit less. Custom On-Hold messaging that is engaging and relevant is just like hanging those screens near the checkout line of Best Buy.

In his article on time perception, Adam Alter explains:

There's still plenty we don't understand about how humans perceive time, but one fact is clear: we don't perceive

time the way clocks portray time, one second at a time, with
each second passing just as quickly as its earlier and later
counterparts.

Sure, nobody likes to wait, but what kind of experience is your company providing for those customers who call in? Is your Caller Experience a good one? Are you speeding up your customer's clock, or slowing it down?

Keep it Current and Fresh

In a study released in January 2010, Consumer Reports revealed that waiting to talk to a live human when calling a company ranked as the second most annoying thing you and I deal with daily. (The first? Hidden fees.)

There's no doubt why. We're all busy. We want to accomplish our goals while taking the least amount of time possible. And waiting while listening to silence is more annoying than being stuck in a traffic jam! (Only #14 on the list.)

In fact, respondents said they would rather scoop dog poop than wait On-Hold! (Don't believe me? Check out the results at Consumer Reports.[9])

As a business, what can you do about this situation? There's always the first thing that comes to mind…Hire more people!

---

[9] http://www.consumerreports.org/cro/magazine-archive/2010/january/shopping/what-bugs-america-most/overview/what-bugs-america-most-ov.htm

That's what most people suggest. And mostly that suggestion probably comes from someone who has never owned his own business. There can never be a 1-1 ratio of employees to customers. It simply is not feasible.

But most helpful folk don't stop to consider that. They just want you to handle their issue right now.

Take your On-Hold time seriously. As seriously as a customer walking in your front door. What are the things you do to make your customer's first impression a great one? Do you hire an interior decorator? Do you keep the customer-visible areas neat and clean? Do you have information for customers to take with them when they walk out the door?

You can do the same thing for customers who call your business.

Make a great first impression by having more than silence On-Hold. An On-Hold message will grab your caller's ear when he first hears it.

You've got my ear...now what?

Now you've got a few short seconds to convince the caller to keep listening. Is it going to be interesting? Or is it going to be about how long you've been in business?

Are you going to tell the caller a story...and make him the star? Or are you going to keep all the stardom to yourself and try to make your business the most important thing in the message. (Hint: customers like to imagine themselves using your product or service to make their lives better. They don't really care that you've been in business since 1942.)

If you want an On-Hold message that will turn angry customers into laughing ones, tell callers about products or services they didn't know you offered, or flat-out sell more products, you better be paying attention to the phone. After you resolve that situation, then let's work on a solution for tailgaters…that's the next most annoying thing on Consumer Report's list!

Are You Listening?

"I'm spending too much time On-Hold," or "Every time I call, I get put On-Hold, and I don't like it!"

You won't often get this kind of straightforward feedback from customers: "I'm spending too much time On-Hold," or "Every time I call, I get put On-Hold, and I don't like it!"

When customers have the guts to speak up and tell you what you're doing wrong, it would be best to listen.

But it takes really listening, not just to what they are saying, but what they are meaning. If someone is calling your company to see whether his order came in, there is a certain expectation that he will have to wait for you to find out if it has arrived.

Yet these same people would say, "I'm spending too much time On-Hold" or "Whatever you do, don't put me On-Hold." So in essence, they are expecting to wait, but they are asking you not to make them wait. Hmmmm….

Have you ever been somewhere, expecting to have a mediocre experience, but you came away surprised at how much you enjoyed it! (I sure have!)

Most people's experience and expectation with being On-Hold is one of frustration, anxiety, and disgust. They've experienced the silence ("Am I still connected?" "Did they hang up on me?"), the radio station ("Exactly the kind of music I don't listen to." "Don't they know this radio station is not tuned in?"), and "Rhapsody in Blue" on repeat.

So what could your customers be saying? They may be telling you that the experience of being On-Hold at your business makes them want to hurl their phone through the window (or some other nearby glass object). They may be telling you that the phone is one area of your business that is not drawing them in to do more business with you.

Have someone unrelated to your company call into your business and get put On-Hold. Have him evaluate the experience. Is it silence? Do you have a message playing but the volume is so loud that you can't understand what's being said? Is it so soft that the sound is dropping out? (Hint: the volume of your On-Hold message should be the same level as your receptionist answering the phone).

Is the radio in tune? One of the hazards of using a radio for your On-Hold is the ease of having the antenna bumped or station changed. (Not to mention that playing the radio On-Hold is illegal[10] in most cases.)

So what kind of experience are you providing for your callers? Is it an environment that is pleasing to your callers?

And if your customers are talking to you about it, are you listening to what they are telling you?

---

[10] http://bmi.com/licensing/faq

And here's an interesting anonymous tool for reporting bad (and good) On-Hold experiences: www.onholdhell.com. Next time you're On-Hold and hating it, check it out.

So what are your callers listening to…and what if you delighted your callers?

Don't Play the Radio!

Have you ever been "invited" to be put On-Hold, and found yourself listening to the static of an unknown radio station? It happened to me recently. I called a prominent, nationwide company's local office, and when I was put On-Hold…I heard a radio station that was just slightly off the channel, resulting in a lot of static. Listening to a static radio station isn't a great way to give me a good feeling about the company.

"Of course," you say, "in your business, you're a lot more tuned into thinking about the On-Hold experience." True. But have you paid attention to what your callers are saying about your On-Hold experience?

Want a real-time view of what callers hate (and like!) to hear while they're On-Hold? Go to http://search.twitter.com, and search for On-Hold. Then call your company. Ask to be put On-Hold, and walk a few minutes in the shoes (or "ears") of your customer. The experience might change you….If it encourages you to start talking to your caller, in his language, and transforming your caller experience, then great!

Anything less, and you're really just tuning static.

Chapter 9
IVR and Auto-Attendant Best Practices

"Please choose from the following six options."

When designing the options for your IVR or Auto-Attendant, make sure they match your customer's expectations. Presenting a caller with four or five clear, concise options will allow him to navigate through your system quickly, without wasting time waiting to hear options he is not interested in.

Using only four or five options will likely take some extra thought on your part to make sure you are expressing the options in a way callers will find helpful and convenient.

Recently, I had an experience with a system concerning options. I was trying to reach one brand division of a large holding company, for tech support on a tool. I found its number on the Support section of its website, which lists the company's eight divisions. However, the Auto-Attendant only listed six divisions! (Two of which sounded *very* similar) And worst of all, the one brand division I wanted wasn't even listed. Now, what was I to do? I guessed, selected option 1, and got lucky that the company combined its tech support in one place!

So, what could the company have done to make its phone options more caller-friendly? If in fact the two support options are combined, it can go ahead and express that in the greeting.

Instead of saying "For Victor, press 1," the company could have easily created "For Victor and Brand X, press 1." Then I would have known which option to choose.

In this case, the company had the choice to include Brand X as a seventh option, to combine it with the first option, or to leave it out all together. Unfortunately, the company chose the last option. With a little more thought, it could have not only kept its options short and concise, but it could have saved me the frustration of having to call back a couple of times to guess the right option!

Repeat the options, with a prompt.

When you have reached the end of your options, allow the caller to repeat, but let the caller know that is what is happening. You can give him the choice to repeat ("To repeat these options, press *"), or you can automatically repeat them (stay on the line to hear these options repeat). Sometimes people do need to hear the options again, and simply to send them to an operator won't serve them or your business the most effectively. No matter what, don't EVER simply disconnect the call after the options are played! That is a great way to make people never call you back!

Let callers know the number of options upfront. ("Please choose from the following six options.")

Another way to manage your caller's expectations is to let him know at the very beginning, how many options you will give him. That would sound like, "Please select from the following six options." This information allows callers to know how long they'll have to listen, and how many choices they need to keep in their heads before they choose a selection.

Always Give the Option Before the Number

As I approached the elevators to head to my fourteenth floor hotel room recently, I was met with the elevator selector pictured here. Someone on the design team of this elevator company felt 100 percent positive that this selector was designed clearly so I would have no trouble at all in choosing whether I wanted to go up or down. You may think so as well.

But look closely...

If you wanted to go Up, do you push the button that the Up arrow is pointing to? Or the button beside the Up arrow? It kinda looks a little circular to me, and that could get frustrating!

Here's what this elevator selector has to do with phone systems. Too often, the Auto-Attendant is set up on the fly by whoever is installing the phone system. Sure, the installer has tried to get the business owner or manager to tell him what options to program, and what to say, but the truth is, the business owner is thinking "Phone System" at that point, not "Caller Experience." See, those are two different parts of the brain!

How many times have you called a phone system that sounds like this: "Thank you for calling XYZ Corp, where we really value your business! If you know your party's four-digit extension, you may enter it at anytime. Please press 1 for Sales. Please press 2 for Service. Please press 3 for Parts. Please press 4 for Accounting. Please press 5 for Human Resources, or press 0 to reach an operator. Press 9 to repeat this message."

That's even hard to write, must less listen to over the phone! And here's why: When you give the number before the option, I have to hold that number in my head while I listen to the option, and I have to analyze whether or not that's the option I need. After listening above, I've got a total of seven options in my head, and they are all jumbled together. Because I'm not calling to push a number…I'm calling to go to a department.

If you list the department first, followed by the option ("To reach sales, press 13") the department name, "clicks" with what I'm looking for in my head, making it a very easy choice to press 1. If I don't need the Sales department, I can simply forget about that option altogether, and move on to the next one.

There's a time to answer the phones with a live person. And there's a time to use an Auto-Attendant. (Do you know which one to use when?)

When you decide to use an Auto-Attendant, make sure the options are clear, and easy for your caller to understand— not confusing like our elevator. If you confuse your callers, they won't know which way is up! (and they will go for the last option they hear by pressing 1"!)

So what does your Auto-Attendant sound like from the caller's perspective?

Put the Most Popular Option First

Sometimes you just have to laugh at the Auto-Attendant and On-Hold messages at some companies. I mean, who are they kidding? Is your call really "very important to us"?

The Caller

By Frank Halliwell[11]

"Good morning! Thanks for calling us!
We're pleased to hear from you!
Your call's important to us
So we've placed you in a queue.

Please find your account number and

---

[11] Frank Halliwell, Jimboomba, Australia, Public Domain

Be sure it is correct.
It's twenty digits long and if you
Mis-type, I'll reject.

I'll lead you through the whole routine
Please use your touch type phone.
Press eight and follow with the hash
After you hear the tone.

If you are a new client here.
Press two, if old, press three.
Press four in case we've done something
With which you disagree!

You have pressed four, please wait a moment
While I transfer you.
And please enjoy, while we play you
A symphony or two!

Our staff are all too busy now
To talk to such as you.
Your call is so important that
We've placed you in a queue."

Time passes and the music lingers
On, and bye and bye.
My cheek and ear go fast asleep,
My wrist gets R.S.I.

But wait! It may be there is hope!
I hear a ringing sound,
At last a human voice is heard
After the runaround!

"Good morning, this is Ladies wear
And may we help somehow?
Complaints?. Oh! Just hang on a tick
I'll transfer you right now!..."

"Good morning! Thanks for calling us!
We're pleased to hear from you!
Your call's important to us
So we've placed you in a queue.

Recently I was researching the features of a customer's phone system at the manufacturer's website, and the manufacturer had this to say about its On-Hold message:

The InterStellar Phone System gives you the opportunity to have music playing while a caller is on hold. Best of all you can insert interruptions during each recording in order to play a message.

You've experienced this kind of On-Hold situation whether or not you remember it. You're On-Hold, listening to the music or messaging, when all the sudden "click." The music is interrupted, and hope springs up within you that your call is going to be answered. Only to have your hopes dashed by the message, "Your call is important to us; please continue to hold."

Can you say, "Disappointment"?

I was On-Hold with a company last week that interrupted its On-Hold music with this reminder that I was On-Hold every ten seconds! Never do this to your callers.

Just because you use an Auto-Attendant doesn't mean it has to be a poor caller experience.

Want to know what your caller's experience is like? Try a Caller Experience Evaluation service. It's like climbing inside your customer's head and hearing your business from his perspective. Very informative!

A recent client who used this service, gave this feedback: "Thanks for getting the report to me as fast as you did. I will be correcting a lot of the concerns you pointed out. Thanks again!"

Don't give your callers the run-around.

Make it easy to reach a live person.

Always. Always. Always give the option for your caller to reach a live person. Make it easy. Don't hide behind your phone system, forcing callers to do things the way *you* want them done. I can guarantee you that at some point, a customer will call with some issue that doesn't fit neatly into your pre-programmed options, and connecting that caller to a live person will resolve the issue with less frustration on his or her part.

You can resolve this situation with the standard press "0" for the operator option, or by some other unique way. ("If you want to reach someone, *anyone*, just press 0, and we'll be happy to talk to you!")

Think about who should take those calls. It depends on your business structure, but consider *not* sending those calls to a receptionist or secretary. Think about it....What this caller needs hasn't been addressed by any of the options in your Auto-Attendant. Do you think the secretary is qualified to handle the caller's request? Likely not.

That doesn't mean route the call to the business owner or president, but at least send those calls to a person (or group of people) who has the power to make things happen, answer in-depth questions, or otherwise generally make customers happy (which is, after all, the point of your business...isn't it?)

Having said that, when calls come in that are simple, but will take more than a minute to answer, have someone designated to receive that call. There may be calls that come in that *can* be handled by the secretary. Have a plan simply to say, "Mrs. Jones will be glad to help you with that. May I transfer you directly to her?"

Always give the option to reach a live person in some way. Your customers will thank you for it!

Repeat the greeting automatically, *or* give the option to your callers.

Set up your Auto-Attendant to repeat the greeting automatically, and if you can't do that, select an option key for callers to press that will replay the message. Callers may miss the option they need the first time, and not realize it until later. Some systems automatically route the call to the operator if you don't press anything. But don't automatically route the call until after the message has repeated at least once.

I've heard Auto-Attendants that disconnect the call if you don't make a selection quickly enough! Talk about not being customer-friendly! A recorded voice saying, "Goodbye," simply because I was thinking about the option I needed, or didn't realize I had reached the end of the menu, is a great way to lose a customer!

Voicemail Etiquette

Speak clearly

The greeting you record on your own voicemail box can be critical to how callers connect with you. Number 1 on the list of things to remember is: Speak Clearly. I've heard dozens of mumbled greetings, garbled recordings, speaking too fast. That is not a great way to start a relationship! Your greeting should be an invitation for people to connect with you. Speak clearly and distinctly. That doesn't mean overly slow or robotic, but you want people to be able to understand you.

Use your name

"Hi. Leave a message" Hmmm, have I reached the right voicemail? Was that really that person's voice I heard? I don't want to leave this message for the wrong person and look like an idiot. Maybe I just won't leave a message at all.

Use your name in your message. It provides confirmation to your callers that they have reached you, and that they're not

on some accidental mis-dial adventure that sends them off into
Generic Voicemail Land.

Use your voice when possible

Second to using your name, your voice most closely
identifies your mailbox. Use it. Record your own greeting.
Don't leave it up to the phone installer, your secretary, or some
person you find on the sidewalk. It's your voicemail, so record
it in your voice! And customize it beyond the default standard
of "You have reached the voicemail of...<insert your name
here>...please leave a message after the tone."

Think of your voicemail not as a hassle, or a pain, but as
a way to multiply your effectiveness. It allows you to be in two
places at once. One, answering calls at your desk, and two, out
where you want or need to be. So use your voice when you
record your voicemail greeting.

Provide alternate means of connecting with you

If another way of reaching you is preferred, you want to
give people the option; it's a great way to let people know how
to reach you. Leave your email address or cell phone. More
than one or two alternate options is probably too many, but it
might be easier to remind people about your email address than
to play phone tag with them only to find out they wanted you to
attach a file and email it to them! Remember, 51 percent of
people are extroverted and would prefer to pick up the phone
and call you, even when an email would be more efficient!

Change it frequently (daily)

Changing your voicemail daily might sound like a chore right now, but what a difference it makes in the connection you're able to provide by updating people about your daily plans. Are you in the office today, but temporarily tied up? Are you out of the office all day, so they shouldn't expect a call back today? Will you be out in the morning, but back in this afternoon? Or are you on permanent vacation? (in which case, maybe voicemail isn't applicable to you! Send me your secret so I can join you!)

I've often appreciated reaching people who have updated their voicemail daily. Most phone systems will let you set a one-button speed dial to connect with your voicemail to change the greeting. Very quick and easy.

One caveat: Don't forget to change your message back after a holiday, vacation, or being away. That's easily solved if you do it every day, but if you forget, it's a little embarrassing that your summer vacation greeting is what callers hear in November!

Night Answer Options

Having your phone system change the greeting when you're closed is a very customer-friendly thing to do.

Think about this scenario: It's 5:05 p.m. You need to order parts, so you pick up the phone, call the parts company, and your call is answered by its Auto-Attendant. It then puts you in queue for the parts department, and you wait. And wait. And wait.

Pretty soon it dawns on you that the parts company probably closed at 5 p.m. Or was it 6 p.m.? You simply don't know! Do you continue to hold, not wanting to lose your place in the queue? Or are you the only fool holding while the phones ring incessantly in an empty building?

The only way to keep *your* customers from experiencing this situation is to use a night answer option. Program it to let your callers know instantly that you are closed. You can then give them options to leave a voicemail, route to specific people's voicemail boxes, or even direct them to the web.

Some systems will enable you to count calls that come in after hours, so you can determine whether adjusting your hours would bring you more business. Don't leave your customers in the dark! If you're closed, let them know, and provide them with ways or times they can engage with you.

Chapter 10
Phones or Social Media?

The Phone as part of your Social Media

Chris Brogan writes about how companies are jumping on the Social Media bandwagon[12] as a customer service tool, while their existing customer infrastructure is in major need of a transformation!

So companies are going to the social media space to reach customers, and rightfully so. But in the rush to meet customers where they're at, those same companies are forgetting that 91 percent of U.S. households have cell phones (Source: CTIA December 2009), and I have never walked into a business that didn't have a landline of some sort.

The telephone as a tool to connect to customers may be the most overlooked "social media" tool there is. I talk to companies almost every day who have no idea what their customers hear when they call. These companies have spent thousands (and sometimes hundreds of thousands) of dollars on marketing and advertising, without considering how the Caller Experience they provide will impact that potential sale.

---

[12] http://www.chrisbrogan.com/it-wont-matter/

So while on one hand, social media is working hard to deliver customer satisfaction, at the same time, the Caller Experience is fighting against its efforts!

I'm all for social media. It's certainly a very valid and current way to reach customers. But it would be a much more effective tool if customers weren't turning to it as a last resort, out of frustration from the Caller Experience!

Fix the leak in your cup before filling it up. Your customers will thank you.

Chapter 11
Make the Call

Why the next thing you should do is pick up the phone.

We've talked about a lot of Caller Experiences, good and bad. And it's easy to criticize mistakes that others make. But if that's all that happens, then reading this book will be a waste of your time.

The only way to create change is to become the change you want to see in others. For that reason, I've included a sixteen-point Caller Experience Checklist in the next section. With this checklist, not only will you know what to do, but you will be able to see easily what you need to change to improve your own Caller Experience! You can download the PDF version of the Caller Experience Checklist at http://prosoundusa.com/checklist.

You should go over this checklist at least once a year to make sure your company is delivering the best experience possible.

And remember to have fun with it! There's no rule that says the Caller Experience has to be dry, dull, and boring. In fact, if your phone system sounds like a "phone system," it probably could use some help!

So pick up your phone, dial your company, and think about what it's like to be your own customer. Because your customers are doing it every day!

Caller Experience Checklist

For Evaluating Your Caller Experience

Use this checklist to evaluate your own Caller Experience. Take notes, and try to identify ways to improve...from the *caller's* perspective.

1. Live Answer

a. Greeting: Is your greeting carefully crafted so it can be delivered in a natural way?

_____

_____

_____

_____

b. Tone: Is the tone welcoming, or do callers feel like they've just interrupted something else?

_____

_____

_____

_____

c. Competency: Does your staff know how to transfer calls, find the right person, place people On-Hold, and generally navigate your phone system with confidence?

_____

_____

_____

_____

    d. Transfer/Hold Etiquette: Do callers get asked whether
       they'd like to be transferred or put On-Hold? Is there an
       opportunity for them to respond? Are they being well
       taken care of?

_____

_____

_____

_____

2. Auto-Attendant

    a. Structure: Are the options ordered correctly? Are your
      most popular options first?

_____

_____

_____

_____

    b. Clarity of Choices: Is it clear where people are going
      when they select an option?

_____

_____

_____

_____

    c. Personality: Does the overall "personality" of your
      Auto-Attendant match the personality of your company?

_____

_____

_____

_____

    d. Number of Options: Try to keep these to four or five, and no more than six.

_____

_____

_____

_____

3. On-Hold Message

    a. Fresh: When was the last time you updated your message?

_____

_____

_____

_____

    b. Relevant: Are you talking about things your customer cares about?

_____

_____

_____

_____

c. Music: Does it fit with the style of your company?

_____

_____

_____

_____

d. Voice: Does the voice fit the image of your company?
Are there ways you could connect this voice to other
parts of your marketing?

_____

_____

_____

_____

e. Content: Do you have enough content? Too much
content?

_____

_____

_____

_____

f. Personality: Does the personality of your On-Hold
message match your company's personality? (Fun,
serious, humorous, etc.?)

_____

_____

_____

_____

g. Length: Is your On-Hold message long enough that it
doesn't repeat too often for callers? Does it contain
enough information?

_____

_____

_____

_____

h. Sound Quality: Is the volume too high or too low? Is the
message clear? Is there static?

_____

_____

_____

_____

Glossary

Jargon

Industry lingo and insider jargon are always fun to use...when you're in the know! But if words or phrases we use are not understood by everyone in the conversation, we can quickly have miscommunications!

That's why we've compiled this brief glossary. To explain some of the terms, slang, and insider jargon that sometimes come too naturally to us tech geeks!

Auto-Attendant/Automated Attendant: An automated attendant (also auto attendant, auto-attendant, AA, or virtual receptionist) allows callers to be automatically transferred to an extension without the intervention of an operator/receptionist.

Blind Transfer: When one person transfers the call to another person or department without passing along any information. This transfer is usually done by pressing "Transfer," then the extension to transfer to, then hanging up. See also **Supervised Transfer**.

Dual Tone Multi Frequency (DTMF): The standard tone-pairs used on telephone terminals for dialing, using in-band signaling. The standards define sixteen tone-pairs (0-9, #, * and

A-F) although most terminals support only twelve of them (0-9, * and #). These tone-pairs are also sometimes referred to as "Touch Tones" (actually a copyrighted trade name held by AT&T). Note that while digital data terminals have the same symbols, ISDN uses "common channel signaling" (over the D channel), and therefore, it does not necessarily generate any tones at all. However, many terminals still generate the tones since they will still be used on occasion to access services (such as voicemail or automated attendant) at the far end using in-band tones.

Hold Message: A service used by businesses and organizations of all sizes to deliver targeted information to their callers waiting on hold or while they are being transferred. Also commonly called Music On-Hold.

IVR: Interactive voice response (IVR) is a technology that allows a computer to interact with humans through the use of voice and DTMF keypad inputs.

Key Telephone System: A system that allows multiple telephones to share multiple pre-determined telephone lines. The system provides indicators to allow the users to understand the status of each line available on a given phone. It is up to the user to provide the intelligence to select an unused line, or answer a ringing line, for example.

PBX: A system that allows multiple telephones to share multiple pre-determined telephone lines. The system provides indicators to allow the users to understand the status of each line available on a given phone. It is up to the user to provide the intelligence to select an unused line, or answer a ringing line, for example.

Primary Rate Interface (PRI): A form of ISDN with twenty-three "B Channels" and one "D channel." All twenty-four channels are on a single cable. Functionally related to T1 telephone circuits.

Queue/Hold Message: A service used by businesses and organizations of all sizes to deliver targeted information to their callers waiting on hold or while they are being transferred. Also commonly called Music On-Hold.

Supervised Transfer: When one person transfers a call to another person or department, but waits for that person or department to answer before hanging up the handset to complete the transfer. This practice allows the original person to pass along any information he or she has about the call or the caller.

T1 Circuit: A common type of digital telephone carrier widely deployed within the U.S., Canada, and Japan. Has twenty-four 64Kbps channels (called DSÆ's). The most common framing scheme for T1 "robs" bits for signaling leaving 56kbps per channel available.

Telco: Telephone Company. Your local telephone service provider. In the twenty-first century, you generally have a choice of Telcos if you are a business in a major metropolitan area in the USA. Competition is coming to the Telecom industry around the world.

About the Author

Chester Hull is a writer, entrepreneur, Caller Experience evangelist, and Director of Client Happiness at Prosound. Prosound helps companies around the globe transform their Caller Experience through custom designed IVR's, call flows, and Queue/Hold messaging. Chester is passionate about spreading the message that phone interactions with companies large and small don't have to be agonizing, and with a little thought and planning, your company can have happy callers!

Chester serves on the Board of Directors of OHMA, the On Hold Messaging Association.

Chester lives in Virginia with his wife and four children. He enjoys mountain biking, camping, technology, and listening to, creating, and mixing sounds of all sorts.

www.ingramcontent.com/pod-product-compliance
Lightning Source LLC
Chambersburg PA
CBHW060625210326
41520CB00010B/1475